KET for Schools DIRECT

CW00497201

Workbook without answers
Sue Ireland and Joanna Kosta

Contents

CAMBRIDGE
UNIVERSITY PRESS

1.1 Where are you from?

Language practice

1 Match the countries to the nationalities.
Then write them in the maps.

0 India	A Venezuelan
1 Kenya	B German
2 Japan	C Indian
3 Peru	D French
4 Germany	E Kenyan
5 Morocco	F Japanese
6 Venezuela	G Peruvian
7 France	H Moroccan

South America

_____

_____

Africa

_____

_____

Europe

_____

_____

Asia

_____*India*_____

_____

2 Write the numbers as words.

0 There are (50) _____*fifty*_____ stars on the American flag.
1 There are (195) _____ countries in the world.
2 India has more than (20) _____ languages.
3 There are (54) _____ countries in Africa.
4 There are (12) _____ stars on the European flag.
5 There are (27) _____ countries in the European Union.
6 There are (3) _____ colours on the French flag.

3 Put the words in the right order.

0 say / you / English / How / do / 'tenho'/ in   *How you do say 'tenho' in English* ?
1 pronounce/ How / do / word / this / you   _____?
2 don't / Sorry, / I / understand   _____.
3 you / please / say / that / again, / Can   _____?
4 mean / What / 'windy'/ does   _____?
5 you / How / do / that / spell   _____?

Exam practice: Speaking Part 1

4 Write your own answers to the questions, then practise saying them.

1 What's your name?   _____
2 Where do you come from?   _____
3 How old are you?   _____
4 Can you spell your surname?   _____
5 What's your phone number?   _____

When do you have English?

Language practice

1 Write the words in the table.

> beginner board chair classmate college diploma desk degree fail
> library pass pupil student table teacher take test university

People	Places to study	Furniture	Exams	Exam verbs
beginner				

2 Complete the crossword.

Across 👉

1 This person has just started learning.
3 You may get this at university.
6 We always _____ exams in the summer.
7 I hope I _____ all my exams this year!
9 You do this when you want to learn.
11 You can put your books on this.
12 A group of students who are studying together.

Down ✍

2 This subject is about the world around us.
4 A child at school.
5 This subject is about painting and drawing.
8 You have to do this subject if you want to be an engineer.
10 You do this if you are a teacher.

3 Complete the email with the correct words.

> ~~homework~~ library teacher test university

To: Alex
Subject: school today

Hi Alex,
You weren't at school today. Are you ill? Mr Jameson gave us LOTS of History **(0)** *homework*! We've got a new Art **(1)** _____. Her name is Miss Evans, and she said I should study Art at **(2)** _____. John talked a lot in the Maths lesson, so he had to go and work in the **(3)** _____. Oh, and we've got a Maths **(4)** _____ tomorrow, so you might want to stay at home again!
Tom

4 Look at the clocks and write the times in two different ways.

0 5:55

1

2 6:30

3

4 8:15

5

0   *five fifty-five*   *five to six*
1   _____   _____
2   _____   _____
3   _____   _____
4   _____   _____
5   _____   _____

2.1 What does she look like?

Language practice

1 Put the letters in the right order.

0 your mother's sister
   n u t a _____aunt_____

1 a boy who has the same parents as you
   b e r t h o r _____

2 your Mum's or Dad's parents
   r g a t n p e s n a d r _____

3 the child of your parent's brother or sister
   i c u o n s _____

4 the brother of one of your parents
   c l u e n _____

5 a girl who has the same parents as you
   t s i r e s _____

2 Look at the pictures and write the correct name next to each description.

0 I'm 74 and I've got grey hair. I'm quite thin. _____Toby_____

1 I'm 18. I'm tall and I've got long dark hair. _____

2 My hair is short and fair. I'm 50 years old. I'm not very tall. _____

3 I've got short dark hair. I'm tall and I'm a bit fat. _____

4 I'm 16. My hair is blonde and long. I'm not very tall. _____

George   Amanda   Debbie   Marina   Toby

3 Write the questions in this interview with the singer Gabriella.

INTERVIEWER: **(0)** _____What is your full name_____ ?
             full / name / is / what / your?
GABRIELLA: Gabriella Cilmi.
INTERVIEWER: **(1)** _____
             from / you / do / where / come?
GABRIELLA: From Melbourne, Australia.
INTERVIEWER: **(2)** _____
             do / you / where / now / live?
GABRIELLA: In London , with my mother.
INTERVIEWER: **(3)** _____
             brothers / and /you / sisters / got / any / have?

GABRIELLA: I've got one brother.
INTERVIEWER: **(4)** _____
             London / in / too / he / is?
GABRIELLA: No, he's in Australia with my dad.
INTERVIEWER: **(5)** _____
             write / songs / all / do / your / you?
GABRIELLA: No, I write some of my songs, but not all.
INTERVIEWER: **(6)** _____
             singers / like / do / which / you?
GABRIELLA: I like lots of different singers, for example Janis Joplin.

Exam practice: Reading and Writing Part 2

4 Read the sentences about Joe's family. Choose the best word (A, B or C) for each space.

0 Everyone in Joe's family has got __A__ eyes.
   (A) blue   B fair   C blonde

1 Joe's brother Tom has _____ brown hair.
   A fat   B short   C old

2 Joe's sister Anna is _____ and very pretty.
   A tall   B high   C long

3 Joe's mother _____ in an office.
   A gets   B works   C does

4 Joe's dad is the same _____ as his mum.
   A time   B year   C age

5 Joe _____ a lot of football with Tom.
   A plays   B practises   C gives

2.2 What does he do?

Language practice

1 Match the jobs to the places and things.

0	police officer	A	hotel	5	hairdresser	F	lorry
1	receptionist	B	classroom	6	shop assistant	G	camera
2	teacher	C	uniform	7	photographer	H	scissors
3	zookeeper	D	animals	8	driver	I	customer
4	actor	E	theatre	9	painter	J	brush

2 Complete the crossword and find the hidden word.

1 Come to me if your teeth hurt.
2 I look after people who are ill.
3 I am in charge of a shop, bank or factory.
4 Flying is my job.
5 I write for a newspaper.
6 If your car has a problem I'll repair it.
7 I grow food for you to eat.
8 My boss asks me to write letters and send emails.

Crossword answers visible:
1. D
2. N
3. M
4. P
5. J
6. M
7. F
8. S

3 Read the article and write the jobs that match the descriptions.

★★★★★★★★★★★★ **A famous family** ★★★★★★★★★★★★★

The Fiennes family are amazing. Jini, a writer and painter, and her husband Mark Fiennes, a photographer, had seven children. Two of their sons, Ralph and Joseph, are well-known actors. Another son, Jacob, is a travel writer and photographer. The fourth son, Magnus, is a musician and also a songwriter. One of their daughters, Sophie, makes documentary films, and their second daughter Martha is a film producer. Sometimes they work together. Ralph stars in several of Martha's films, and Magnus wrote the music for one of them.

Perhaps it's not surprising that a half-cousin of the family is the famous explorer Ranulph Fiennes. He travels all over the world, and he also writes books about his adventures. At the moment he is planning to climb Mount Everest for a second time.

0 Someone who paints pictures as their job. _painter_
1 Someone who takes photographs for their job. _____
2 Someone who appears in films. _____
3 Someone who writes about places they travel to. _____
4 Someone who plays music. _____
5 Someone who writes songs. _____
6 Someone who helps to make films. _____
7 Someone who visits new places a long way away. _____

★★

4 Choose the correct verbs to complete the sentences.

0 Sam's dad *(plays)* / *is playing* tennis with his colleagues on Saturdays.
1 Amy's mother *doesn't work* / *isn't working* at weekends.
2 All Tom's friends *read* / *are reading* the new *Harry Potter* book at the moment.
3 Emily *sends* / *is sending* lots of text messages to her friends every day.
4 'Where are Mike and Sara?' 'They *play* / *are playing* on the computer.'
5 Mum usually *cooks* / *is cooking* fish for dinner on Fridays.

Language practice

1 Underline the word that doesn't belong in each group. How is this word different?

0 tennis	football	baseball	<u>computer game</u>	*It's not a sport.*
1 beach	shopping centre	park	train	_____
2 café	shop	snack bar	restaurant	_____
3 cinema	stadium	theatre	house	_____
4 picnic	nightclub	lunch	barbecue	_____
5 film	magazine	television	DVD	_____

2 Match the problems to the suggestions.

0 It's really hot in here
1 This game's boring.
2 We need more people for the match on Sunday.
3 I'm thirsty.
4 I'm bored. Let's go out tonight.
5 This homework is so difficult!

A Shall we play another one?
B Me too. There's a café over there. Let's get a drink.
C What about looking for help on the internet?
D What about asking Sue and Ken to play?
E OK. How about going to the cinema?
F Yeah, let's open a window.

3 Look at the profiles and complete the dialogues by suggesting an activity.

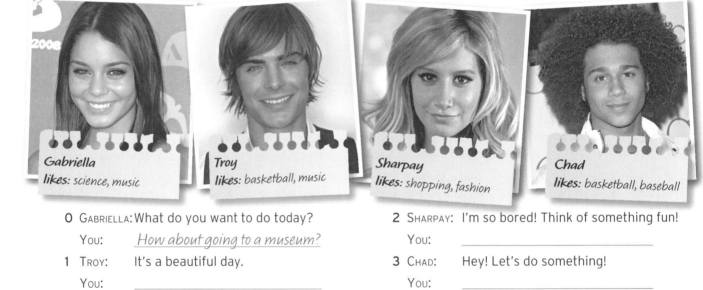

Gabriella
likes: science, music

Troy
likes: basketball, music

Sharpay
likes: shopping, fashion

Chad
likes: basketball, baseball

0 GABRIELLA: What do you want to do today?
  You: *How about going to a museum?*
1 TROY: It's a beautiful day.
  You: _____

2 SHARPAY: I'm so bored! Think of something fun!
  You: _____
3 CHAD: Hey! Let's do something!
  You: _____

Exam practice: Reading and Writing Part 2

4 Read the sentences about going to the beach. Choose the best word (A, B or C) for each space.

0 My best friend is __A__ Jack.
  (A) called   B said   C known
1 If the _____ is good, Jack and I usually go to the beach on our bikes.
  A time   B weather   C sky
2 We _____ a lot of time surfing.
  A spend   B pass   C stay

3 Sometimes we _____ a game of volleyball with our friends.
  A do   B make   C have
4 Afterwards Jack and I are _____ so we get a drink at a snack bar.
  A hungry   B thirsty   C full
5 Jack's Mum often invites me to stay for _____ with them.
  A food   B meal   C dinner

3.2 Can you bring some drinks?

Language practice

1 Look at the text message. Write the sentences that mean:

1 Be on time. _____
2 Remember my party. _____
3 Don't come alone. _____

> Don't forget my party tonight. Bring a friend. Don't be late!
>
> Cristina
>
> xx

2 Complete the article with these words. Some words need *don't*.

0	_Ask_ your parents first if it's OK to have the party.		ask
1	_____ a good date – people usually like Friday or Saturday night.	**How to have a good party!**	ask
2	_____ your friends – you can phone them or make invitations.		buy
3	_____ people you don't know.		choose
4	_____ your friends to bring lots of food and drink.		forget
5	_____ some paper plates and cups so it's easy to clean up!		invite
6	_____ the house and put up some balloons and coloured lights.		play
7	_____ to tell your neighbours about the party (and maybe invite them!).		tell
8	_____ your favourite music and have fun!		tidy

3 Look at the cartoons and write what the people are saying.

0 _Can you_ pass me the orange juice?

1 _____ open the door for you?

2 Where is John? _____ call him?

3 _____ buy it for me, please?

Exam practice: Reading and Writing Part 7

4 Complete these emails. Write ONE word for each space.

To: Jane
Subject: Birthday

Hi Jane,
It's (0) _my_ birthday this weekend, so I'm having a party (1) _____ Friday night. Would you like
(2) _____ come? I'm having a disco and inviting lots of friends to my house. The party starts (3) _____ 7 o'clock.
I'm asking everyone to bring some food, so (4) _____ you bring some snacks (5) _____ crisps?
Love from
Ben

To: Ben
Subject: Re: Birthday

Hi Ben,
Thanks (6) _____ inviting me to your party. It sounds fun! What time (7) _____ it finish? And
(8) _____ it OK if my sister comes too?
I'm (9) _____ shopping tomorrow, so I'll get some snacks. (10) _____ I buy some drinks too?
See you soon!
Jane

4.1 I just got a T-shirt

Language practice

1 Look at the store guide. Where can you buy the things in the list?

0 a CD _in the music department on the ground floor_

1 a football game _____

2 a pair of gloves for your Mum _____

3 a packet of biscuits _____

4 a television _____

5 a tennis racket _____

6 some socks for your Dad _____

7 a desk _____

8 a cup of coffee _____

HARDY'S DEPARTMENT STORE FLOOR GUIDE	
THIRD FLOOR:	Furniture Electrical goods Men's clothes
SECOND FLOOR:	Children's clothes Toys Computers
FIRST FLOOR:	Women's clothes Coffee bar
GROUND FLOOR:	Books Music Customer information
LOWER GROUND FLOOR:	Food Sports

2 Complete the conversation with the words *colours, help, much, size, take* and *try*.

SHOP ASSISTANT: Can I **(0)** _help_ you?

CUSTOMER: What **(1)** _____ is this T-shirt?

SHOP ASSISTANT: It's small.

CUSTOMER: Can I **(2)** _____ it on?

SHOP ASSISTANT: Sure. The changing room's over there.

CUSTOMER: Have you got any other **(3)** _____?

SHOP ASSISTANT: Yes, we've got it in blue and red.

CUSTOMER: I will **(4)** _____ the red one.

SHOP ASSISTANT: OK. You can pay at the cash desk over there.

CUSTOMER: How **(5)** _____ is it?

SHOP ASSISTANT: It was £10, but now it's only £4.

CUSTOMER: Great.

Exam practice: Reading and Writing Part 8

3 Read the email and the advertisement for a new shopping centre.
Fill in the information in Beth's notes.

Opening on
Saturday 21st June, at 9.00!

**High Cross
SHOPPING CENTRE**

Over 80 shops and Gino's Café
– great for snacks!

Bring your friends by car or bus
(the 14 from the town centre).

To: Beth
Subject: High Cross

Hi Beth,

Let's go and have a look at High Cross on the day it opens! You can get a bus from town. I'm catching the 27 from here. Don't forget your big bag! I'll wait for you in their café at 10.15.

Love, Emma

BETH'S NOTES

Name of shopping centre: **(0)** _High Cross_

Day to meet Emma: **(1)** _____

Time: **(2)** _____ a.m.

Meeting place: **(3)** _____

Bus number: **(4)** _____

Bring: **(5)** _____

Language practice

1 Look at the picture of the bedroom and then choose
the correct words to complete the sentences.

0 There *is* / *are* a desk *next to* / *behind* the window.

1 There *is* / *are* a computer *under* / *on* the desk.

2 There *is* / *are* some books and CDs *on* / *in* the shelf.

3 There *is* / *are* a lamp *under* / *next to* the bed.

4 There *is* / *are* a ball *under* / *on* the bed.

5 There *is* / *are* some posters *in* / *on* the walls.

6 There *is* / *are* a guitar *under* / *behind* the door.

7 There *is* / *are* some clothes *in* / *next to* the wardrobe.

Exam practice: Reading and Writing Part 4

2 Read the article about living in an unusual house. Are the sentences below
'Right' (A) or 'Wrong' (B)? If there is not enough information to answer 'Right' (A)
or 'Wrong' (B), choose 'Doesn't say' (C).

Jonty, 14, Annabel, 12, and Dominic, 10, live in a four-storey house in an expensive part of London. The house was built by their father, Sean Harper, who is a well-known architect. 'I think the house is great,' said Annabel. 'It's very different from all the other houses in the street, and I like that.'

'The kitchen is the best,' says Dominic. 'At first we had it downstairs but then Dad moved it upstairs. It's really warm and comfortable and we spend lots of time in there. But I'd like to change our bedroom. It's under the ground and not much light comes through.'

There's one thing Jonty would like to change too. 'The upstairs part of the house is very noisy,' he explains. 'We have metal stairs, and the sound of people going up and down in the morning wakes me up. Also it hurts a lot when you fall down them because there's no carpet!'

The children all say that they like having a dad who is an architect. 'It's good fun when he makes houses and then we go and visit them,' says Annabel. 'The worst thing about it is that he often works late at the office and then we don't see him.'

0 Jonty, Annabel and Dominic live in an apartment.

    A Right   (B) Wrong   C Doesn't say

1 Sean Harper bought the house from a well-known architect.

    A Right   B Wrong   C Doesn't say

2 Sean Harper moved the kitchen upstairs because he wanted to make it bigger.

    A Right   B Wrong   C Doesn't say

3 Dominic thinks their bedroom is too dark.

    A Right   B Wrong   C Doesn't say

4 Jonty says it is difficult to sleep in the house in the mornings.

    A Right   B Wrong   C Doesn't say

5 Jonty asked his father to put a carpet on the stairs.

    A Right   B Wrong   C Doesn't say

6 Annabel enjoys visiting the houses that her Dad builds.

    A Right   B Wrong   C Doesn't say

7 Annabel spends a lot of time with her father in the evenings.

    A Right   B Wrong   C Doesn't say

5.1 We haven't got any milk

Language practice

1 Match the words with the descriptions.

0 This fruit is yellow and sweet.
1 This is the first meal of the day.
2 You use this to cut your food.
3 Potatoes, carrots and onions are examples of these.
4 Some people like to put this in their coffee.
5 You make this with two pieces of bread.
6 These are usually red and you can buy them fresh or in a can.

A a sandwich
B vegetables
C a knife
D breakfast
E milk
F tomatoes
G a banana

2 Look at the picture of the fridge and complete the sentences with *is some*, *are some*, *isn't any* and *aren't any*.

0 There *'s some* cheese.
1 There _____ lemons.
2 There _____ meat.
3 There _____ grapes.
4 There _____ butter.
5 There _____ oranges.

3 Use the words in the box to complete the conversation.

any   any   ~~Are~~   aren't   many   much   some

JESS: So, what have we got in the fridge?
(0) _Are_ there any apples?

KATIE: No, there (1) _____.

JESS: OK. How (2) _____ milk is there?

KATIE: Just two cartons.

JESS: Right, and have we got (3) _____ lemons?

KATIE: Yes, we have, we've got three.

JESS: That's good. How (4) _____ cartons of orange juice are there?

KATIE: Orange juice? There isn't (5) _____ orange juice.

JESS: OK, we can buy (6) _____ when we go shopping.

Exam practice: Reading and Writing Part 3 (a)

4 Complete the five conversations. Choose A, B or C.

0 Would you like some coffee?
A I agree.
B Yes, please.
C Yes, I do.

1 I'll make some sandwiches for lunch.
A Is there some for you?
B Would you like some help?
C What is it made of?

2 How much bread have we got?
A There's one here for you.
B There's lots in the kitchen.
C There aren't any left.

3 What fruit shall I buy?
A I'm afraid I can't.
B It's over there.
C I really don't mind.

4 Please clean the kitchen when you finish.
A Don't worry, I will!
B Sorry, I haven't got any.
C Yes, here you are.

5 I don't know what to cook tonight!
A Well, what's in the fridge?
B OK. Do you mind if I eat?
C Really? Will it be soon?

5.2 Are you ready to order?

Language practice

1 Find eight types of food and drink.

0 S *alad*
1 V_____
2 P_____
3 C_____
4 I_____
5 P_____
6 L_____
7 C_____
8 O_____R_____

V	E	G	E	T	A	B	L	E	S
S	D	A	T	B	M	X	A	S	M
P	A	S	T	A	R	M	M	W	T
B	L	E	M	O	N	A	D	E	B
S	J	C	N	C	H	I	P	S	R
A	L	C	O	L	A	U	N	T	C
I	C	E	C	R	E	A	M	S	X
O	N	I	O	N	R	I	N	G	S
H	F	P	I	Z	Z	A	E	R	A
S	A	L	A	D	F	A	S	T	Q

2 Find the word that does not belong for each part of the menu.

Snacks

Soup	Sandwiches	Ice cream	Fruit juice	Hot drinks
vegetable	egg	banana	pineapple	cola
omelette	cheese	strawberry	mango	tea
chicken	cake	burger	cream	chocolate
onion	ham	lemon	orange	coffee

3 Add one word in each space to complete the conversation in a restaurant.

WAITER: Are you (0) __ready__ to order?

CUSTOMER: Yes, please. I'd (1) _____ a pizza, please, with ham and mushrooms.

WAITER: OK. Do you (2) _____ any chips with that?

CUSTOMER: No, thank you, but (3) _____ I have a green salad, please?

WAITER: Of course. Anything to drink?

CUSTOMER: Yes, I'll (4) _____ an apple juice, please.

WAITER: And what (5) _____ a dessert?

CUSTOMER: How (6) _____ is the ice cream?

WAITER: It's £3.50.

CUSTOMER: OK, a chocolate ice cream, please.

Exam practice:
Reading and Writing Part 6

4 Read the descriptions of some words about restaurants. What is the word for each one? The first letter is already there. There is one space for each other letter in the word.

0 This tells you what food you can buy in a restaurant.   m _e_ _n_ _u_

1 If you order soup, it will come in this.

   b __ __ __

2 This is the person who brings your food to you.

   w __ __ __ __ __

3 A main course usually includes some of these.

   v __ __ __ __ __ __ __ __ __

4 You pay this before you leave a restaurant.

   b __ __ __

5 You can book this at some restaurants.

   t __ __ __ __

Entertainment

6.1 They make him laugh

Language practice

1 Complete the crossword and find the hidden word.

1 This is Brad Pitt's job.

2 The opposite of interesting.

3 An exciting kind of film.

4 You laugh a lot when you watch this kind of film.

5 This kind of film is all about love.

6 This kind of film is not about the real world.

2 Put the letters in the right order to complete the sentences.

0 I watched a very ____strange____ science fiction film last night.   TASEGRN

1 Some films are very sad and make you _____.   RCY

2 Adventure films are usually very _____.   CETINIXG

3 Maddie didn't like that _____ because it was too scary!   RITELRHL

4 I loved that film. It was _____!   RUDOFWNEL

3 Choose the correct pronouns to complete the dialogue.

Right, I've got **(0)** my / mine tickets.

And I've got **(1)** my / mine. Anna, have you got **(2)** your / yours?

(3) Your / yours seat is here, next to **(4)** my / mine.

Thanks. Becky's coming in a minute. She's just phoning **(5)** her / hers mum.

Can I have some popcorn?

I'll ask Becky. It's **(6)** her / hers.

Exam practice: Reading and Writing Part 7

4 Complete these emails. Write ONE word for each space.

To: Sara

☰▾ Subject: Saturday

Hi Sara,

How **(0)** _are_ you? Would you **(1)** _____ to come to the cinema **(2)** _____ me on Saturday? There's **(3)** _____ good comedy film on then. It's called *Funny Bones* and it starts **(4)** _____ 8 o'clock. The cinema is **(5)** _____ to the swimming pool so we can swim before the film starts **(6)** _____ you want to.

Love,

Lauren

To: Lauren

☰▾ Subject: Re: Saturday

Hi Lauren,

(7) _____ sounds great! **(8)** _____ we meet outside the pool? I love comedy films – they make **(9)** _____ laugh.

See you on Saturday. Don't forget **(10)** _____ swimming things!

Love,

Sara

12

6.2   Can you play the guitar?

Language practice

1 Find four instruments and three kinds of music in this word snake.

uvhpianolsholpopijebudrumsjiookrockfnddethguitariadehiphopetlviolinlouv

2 Complete the sentences with the correct modals.

can't   ~~could~~   don't have to   had to

0   Mozart ___could___ play the piano beautifully when he was 6 years old.

1   When I was young, I _____ play the piano, but I hated it!

2   Mike _____ play the guitar very well.

3   You _____ practice every day!

Exam practice: Reading and Writing Part 1

3 Which notice (A–H) says this (1–5)? For questions 1–5, choose the correct letter A–H.

0   You can buy a ticket online. ___H___

1   Anyone can have music classes here. _____

2   This instrument is for you to look at only. _____

3   You can come and listen to music here at the weekend. _____

4   If you are visiting with your teacher, you must not come in through this door. _____

5   You may be able to buy a keyboard here for a low price. _____

A   *Sorry, no music lessons today, the teacher is ill.*

B   GUITAR FOR SALE, NEARLY NEW, GOOD PRICE. CALL TONY – 07584-672456

C   **Fullford Museum**
Children! Please do not play this piano.

D   **The Music Centre**
All instruments half price!
Sale ends this weekend!

E   Piano and Singing Lessons
Children and Adults
All levels

F   **GREEN PARK**
CONCERTS HERE SAT AND SUN 2–5 P.M.
TICKETS £6.00

G   **Tilbury Museum of Music**
School groups, please use other entrance

H   **Harlow Music Festival**
For tickets call 05784-82377,
or visit our website

7.1 I love these boots!

Language practice

1 Put the letters in the right order and write the correct words next to the pictures.

T L E B

W A T S E R E

C O T R A N I A

R S U S O T R E

K R I T S

S T O B O

E J A N S

S E S R D

0 ___belt___   **1** _____   **2** _____   **3** _____

4 _____   **5** _____   **6** _____   **7** _____

2 Choose the correct words to complete the sentences.

0 Put your boots on to go out in the snow, *so* / *or* you'll get cold feet.
1 Jeans are fine for going out with friends, *but* / *because* you can't wear them to a wedding.
2 Sam needs a belt *so* / *because* his new school trousers are too big.
3 Jane wears warm clothes *when* / *but* she goes skating.
4 Take your raincoat *so* / *if* you want to keep dry.
5 There was a dirty mark on Jan's dress, *or* / *so* she put on a skirt and sweater instead.

Exam practice: Reading and Writing Part 8

3 Read the information about a fashion show and the email. Fill in the information in Jenna's notes.

Fashion Show
Saturday/Sunday August 23/24 @ 7.30 pm
Jubilee Hall
Tickets £ 3.50 at the door
or £ 3.00 from Palmer's Store

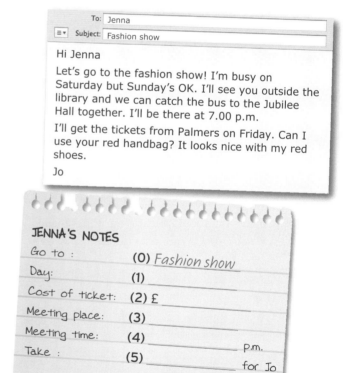

To: Jenna
Subject: Fashion show

Hi Jenna

Let's go to the fashion show! I'm busy on Saturday but Sunday's OK. I'll see you outside the library and we can catch the bus to the Jubilee Hall together. I'll be there at 7.00 p.m.

I'll get the tickets from Palmers on Friday. Can I use your red handbag? It looks nice with my red shoes.

Jo

JENNA'S NOTES
Go to :   (0) *Fashion show*
Day: (1) _____
Cost of ticket: (2) £ _____
Meeting place: (3) _____
Meeting time: (4) _____ p.m.
Take :   (5) _____ for Jo

7.2 He enjoys being in the parade

Language practice

1 Complete the article with these words.

children   clothes   ~~enjoy~~   festival   fireworks   food   homes   lights   luck   presents   visitors

Diwali

✳✳✳✳✳✳✳✳✳✳✳✳✳✳✳✳✳✳✳✳✳✳✳✳✳✳✳✳✳✳✳✳✳   ✳

At the end of October, Hindus all over the world
(0) _enjoy_ getting together for the **(1)** _____
of Diwali. People start cleaning their **(2)** _____
several weeks before Diwali. They put **(3)** _____
round all the windows because they believe this
brings good **(4)** _____ They put on new
(5) _____ and cook lots of special **(6)** _____,
ready for **(7)** _____.

Diwali is very popular with **(8)** _____ because
they can watch **(9)** _____ and people give them
(10) _____.

✳✳

2 Complete the sentences about special days with *in, on* or *at*.

0 Christmas Day is __on__ the 25th of December.

1 _____ New Year's Eve we eat dinner with our families _____ 8 o'clock _____ the evening. Then we go to the Main Square and _____ midnight we eat 12 grapes.

2 Cinco Mayo is a Mexican festival _____ the beginning of May.

3 _____ April Fools' Day in Britain people play tricks on each other.

4 The Notting Hill Carnival takes place _____ August. The children's parade is _____ the Sunday and the main parade is the next day, _____ the afternoon.

5 Are you coming to my birthday party? It's _____ 6 o'clock _____ Saturday.

Exam practice: Reading and Writing Part 9

3 Read this email from your English friend Susie.

To: _____
Subject: Special days

Hi,
Please tell me about your favourite festival.
Who is with you? What do you eat? Why do
you like it?
Susie

4 Write Susie an email. Answer the questions.
Write 25-35 words.

_____
_____
_____
_____
_____
_____
_____
_____
_____
_____

Look after yourself

8.1 You might have the flu

Language practice

1 Find eleven parts of the body.

0 B *ack*

1 F _____	6 M _____
2 H _____	7 N _____
3 A _____	8 H _____
4 S _____	9 F _____
5 E _____	10 E _____

B	A	C	K	F	O	O	T
B	U	O	K	F	G	X	S
H	A	N	D	A	R	M	T
F	G	D	S	C	O	L	O
H	C	O	I	E	S	E	M
E	A	R	L	D	T	Y	A
A	M	O	U	T	H	E	C
D	N	O	S	E	E	G	H

2 Match the problems to the suggestions.

0 I don't feel very well and I've got a temperature.
1 I've hurt my arm. I can't move it.
2 I feel tired all the time.
3 I've got a pain in my stomach and I feel sick.
4 I can't see the board in the classroom.
5 John rides his bike too fast.

A You shouldn't eat anything. You should just drink water.
B He should be careful. He might have an accident.
C You shouldn't stay up so late.
D You may need glasses.
E I think it might be broken.
F I think you might have the flu.

3 Use the words to make sentences to complete the dialogues.

1 A: (sorry / can't come / piano lesson this evening)
I'm sorry, I can't come to my piano lesson this evening.
B: Oh not again! Why not?
A: (fall off / skateboard / hurt / hand)
_____.

2 A: (ring the dentist / please Mum? / can't go / appointment tomorrow.)
_____.
B: Why not? What's the matter?
A: (not / feel well. / temperature.)
_____.

3 A: (sorry Mr Straw / couldn't do / Maths homework last night)
_____.
B: Really? What happened?
A: (eat / fish / feel sick / afterwards)
_____.

4 A: (can't help / clean car today / Dad)
_____.
B: Why? What's wrong?
A: (bad pain / back)
_____.

Exam practice: Reading and Writing Part 6

4 Read the descriptions of some words about health and the body. What is the word for each one? The first letter is already there. There is one space for each other letter in the word.

0 You may need to stay here if you are very ill.
hospital
1 The doctor will give you this to make you feel better.   m _ _ _ _ _ _ _
2 When you have this you feel hot and unwell.
t _ _ _ _ _ _ _ _ _

3 Before you see the doctor you must call and make this.   a _ _ _ _ _ _ _ _ _ _
4 You might get a pain here if you eat bad food.
s _ _ _ _ _ _
5 This person helps the doctor look after you.
n _ _ _ _

8.2 If you win the race...

Language practice

1 Write the sports in the table. Then add some more sports.

~~football~~   karate   skiing   swimming   surfing   tennis   volleyball

water sports	winter sports	team sports	individual sports
		football	

2 Choose the correct words to complete the sentences.

0 I only enjoy horse riding when the horse walks *slow* / *slowly.*

1 Snowboarding is quite a *dangerous* / *dangerously* sport.

2 My team didn't play very *good* / *well* today.

3 George is a very *quick* / *quickly* swimmer.

4 He smiled *happy* / *happily* when he won the match.

5 You have to be very *careful* / *carefully* when you go climbing.

6 Fishing is quite a *slow* / *slowly* sport.

3 Complete the sentences with the correct forms of the verbs.

0    **1**    **2**    **3**

0 If we ___win___ (win) the next game, we ___'ll be___ (be) the champions!

1 You _____ (not be) healthy if you _____ (spend) all your time watching TV!

2 If you _____ (keep) trying, you _____ (get) better!

3 You _____ (be) OK if you _____ (swim) fast!

Exam practice: Reading and Writing Part 2

4 Read the sentences about Roger Federer. Choose the best word (A, B or C) for each space.

0 Roger Federer is an excellent tennis ___A___.
   (A) player   B member   C customer

1 Roger's parents _____ him how to play tennis.
   A learned   B taught   C worked

2 Roger was good at other sports, but he _____ tennis as his job.
   A got   B made   C chose

3 Roger is one of the _____ tennis stars ever.
   A widest   B greatest   C highest

4 Like many other tennis stars, Roger can _____ the ball hard.
   A hit   B give   C catch

5 Roger still _____ his tennis for about four hours every day.
   A spends   B tries   C practises

9.1 It's bigger than a cat

Language practice

1 Put the letters in the right order to make some animals. Then use the highlighted letters to make another animal.

0 REAB   _b e a r_   3 NIOL   _ _ _ _ ▪

1 RHESO   ▪ _ _ _ _   4 RAPROT   ▪ _ _ _ _ _ ▪

2 MACEL   _ ▪ _ ▪ ▪   5 RIGET   _ _ _ ▪ _

2 Complete the sentences with the comparative forms of the adjectives.

0 A giraffe is _taller_ (**tall**) than an elephant.

1 I think fish are _____ (**interesting**) than insects.

2 Tigers are _____ (**dangerous**) than bears.

3 Crocodiles are _____ (**good**) swimmers than elephants.

4 A mouse is _____ (**small**) than a dog.

5 Tigers are _____ (**fast**) runners than elephants.

3 Complete the text with the comparative or superlative form of the adjectives.

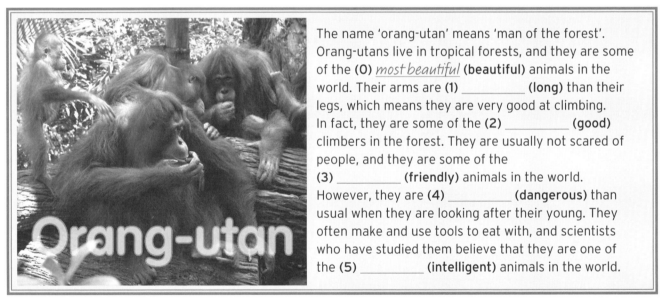

The name 'orang-utan' means 'man of the forest'. Orang-utans live in tropical forests, and they are some of the (0) _most beautiful_ (**beautiful**) animals in the world. Their arms are (1) _____ (**long**) than their legs, which means they are very good at climbing. In fact, they are some of the (2) _____ (**good**) climbers in the forest. They are usually not scared of people, and they are some of the (3) _____ (**friendly**) animals in the world. However, they are (4) _____ (**dangerous**) than usual when they are looking after their young. They often make and use tools to eat with, and scientists who have studied them believe that they are one of the (5) _____ (**intelligent**) animals in the world.

Orang-utan

Exam practice: Reading and Writing Part 3 (a)

4 Complete the five conversations.

0 How are you?
  A I'm Veronika.
  Ⓑ I'm fine.
  C I'm ready.

1 Will you take the dog for a walk?
  A No he won't.
  B I'm just going.
  C He doesn't want it.

2 There's a snake in the garden!
  A I don't believe you.
  B How much is it?
  C I'll think about it.

3 Did you enjoy your riding lesson?
  A I never did.
  B No thank you.
  C Not really.

4 I won this goldfish at the festival.
  A What is it doing?
  B Where did we put it?
  C How did you do that?

5 I'm afraid you can't see the lions today.
  A That's too bad.
  B Sorry they're late.
  C I don't agree.

It's going to rain

Language practice

1 Complete the crossword

Across ☞

1 People grow food and keep animals in this.
2 You can skate on this.
4 There may be snow on the top of this.
6 This is bigger than a village but smaller than a city.
8 This is hot, and plants need it to make them grow.
9 You need an umbrella in this.

Down ☟

1 This has a lot of trees, and it is bigger than a wood.
3 These may be white or grey, and you see them in the sky.
5 This comes before the winter.
7 This weather is good for flying kites.

2 Make sentences using *going to*.

0 Look at those black clouds. (It / rain)   *It's going to rain.*

1 I can hear thunder. (There / be / a storm) _____

2 It's very windy. (I / go / sailing) _____

3 The weather forecast says (it / be / a sunny day) _____

4 (It / not rain / so we / spend / the day on the beach) _____

5 The sky is very cloudy. (it / rain / ?) _____

Exam practice: Reading and Writing Part 3 (b)

3 Complete the conversation between Matt and his mother about going to Australia. What does Matt say to his mother? For questions 1–5, mark the correct letter A–H.

Mum: How's your packing going Matt?
Matt: (0) _B_
Mum: Australia's hot and sunny. You won't need any sweaters.
Matt: (1) ____
Mum: I'm sure six will be enough. There will be lots on sale over there.
Matt: (2) ____
Mum: I'm not sure but take it because it'll be useful in the car.
Matt: (3) ____
Mum: What about your swimming things for the beach?
Matt: (4) ____
Mum: Don't worry. I'm sure you can rent one.
Matt: (5) ____
Mum: Great idea!

A Yes, I guess there'll be a lot of driving.
B OK, but I really need some help.
C OK. Can I use my Playstation on the plane?
D How many have you got?
E I've packed them but what about my surfboard?
F I know, I'll buy one there – an Australian surfboard will be so cool!
G I think they'll be too expensive.
H And what about these T-shirts?

10.1) What are we doing on Saturday?

Language practice

1 Write the correct word next to each picture. Be careful - there are too many words!

book	comb	flight ticket	gloves	guide book	knives and forks
passport	plate	shampoo	skis	sleeping bag	soap	summer clothes
swimming costume	tent	~~toothbrush~~	toothpaste	towel	warm sweater

0 _toothbrush_   **1** _____   **2** _____   **3** _____   **4** _____   **5** _____

6 _____   **7** _____   **8** _____   **9** _____   **10** _____   **11** _____

2 Complete Ella's email with the present continuous forms of the verbs in the box.

come
drive
fly
~~go~~
leave
meet
pack
stay

To: Rowan

Subject: re: holiday

Hi Rowan,

I'm sorry, I can't come out this evening because we **(0)** _'re going_ on holiday tomorrow, so I **(1)** _____ my suitcase tonight. We **(2)** _____ at 5 o'clock in the morning! We **(3)** _____ to the airport in Dad's car, and then we **(4)** _____ to the south of France. My aunt and uncle **(5)** _____ with us, too. They **(6)** _____ us at the airport, and they **(7)** _____ in the same hotel as us. I can't wait!
See you when I get back.
Love, Ella.

Exam practice: Reading and Writing Part 8

3 Read the information about the school trip and the email message. Fill in the information in Jane's notes.

To: Jane

Subject: re: School trip

Jane – you missed the meeting about the school trip. The date's the same, but it's more expensive now – £150. That's because we're doing sailing instead of climbing. The climbing teacher won't be there when we go. We're leaving at 8.00 a.m. so we have to be at school at 7.45 a.m. Don't be late!

School Camping Trip
to Monmouth

From 24th – 28th June

£120 per person

Special activity – climbing

We have tents for everyone but you must bring your own sleeping bag.

JANE'S NOTES

School trip to: _Monmouth_

Price: **(1)** £_____

Leave on: **(2)** _____

Meet at: **(3)** _____

Special activity: **(4)** _____

Take: **(5)** _____

10.2 The buses are too crowded

Language practice

1 Cross out the words that can't be used with the verb.

0 catch	A a bus	B a train	C ~~a bicycle~~
1 miss	A a boat	B a motorbike	C a plane
2 ride	A a train	B a bicycle	C a motorbike
3 drive	A a coach	B a train	C a boat
4 fly	A a helicopter	B a taxi	C a plane
5 sail	A a tram	B a boat	C a ship

2 Write *too much, too many*, or *not enough* and the correct noun next to each picture.

flies   money   people   ~~rain~~   time

0 *too much rain*   **1** _____   **2** _____   **3** _____   **4** _____

3 Complete the sentences with these adjectives.

big   expensive   fast   hot   late   ~~sweet~~   tired

0 I made a cake but nobody liked it because it wasn't ___*sweet*___ enough.

1 My mum didn't buy me the trainers because they were too _____.

2 I missed the bus because I left the house too _____.

3 Our house is nice but it isn't really _____ enough for all of us.

4 I was too _____ to do my homework yesterday so I'll do it today.

5 I'd like to be in my school swimming team but I am not _____ enough.

Exam practice: Reading and Writing Part 5

4 Read the article about holidays. Choose the best word (A, B or C) for each space.

HOLIDAYS

In Britain a hundred years ago, only very rich people **(0)** _could_ go on holiday. Travelling was very expensive, and most people didn't have **(1)** _____ money to go away and stay in **(2)** _____ hotel.

In the 1960s, holiday camps near the sea **(3)** _____ popular. They didn't cost much, and people didn't **(4)** _____ to travel very far to enjoy a week of fun by the sea.

By the 1980s, it was much **(5)** _____ to fly than ever before. A lot of people were able to travel to **(6)** _____ countries for the first time for **(7)** _____ holidays. For British people, a week on the beach is **(8)** _____ the most popular type of holiday.

0	A can	B could	C must
1	A enough	B many	C more
2	A one	B the	C a
3	A became	B become	C becoming
4	A need	B should	C may
5	A cheap	B cheaper	C cheapest
6	A other	B others	C another
7	A his	B its	C their
8	A already	B still	C yet

11.1) Have you been there?

Language practice

1 Match the descriptions to the places.

0 You can buy stamps here. ———————   A a factory
1 People lived in these in the past.   B a bridge
2 They use machines to make things here.   C an office
3 You go here to watch sport.   D a castle
4 You use this to go over a river.   E a stadium
5 A lot of people work in these.   F a post office

2 Jake is going to New York. Look at his list of things to do, then complete the sentences.

Things to do

0 pack my bag	✔	
1 take books back to the library	✔	
2 check the time of the flight	✘	
3 change my money at the bank	✔	
4 look online for places to visit	✘	
5 phone Steve	✔	
6 finish all my homework	✘	

0 He *has packed his bag.*
1 He _____
2 He _____
3 He _____
4 He _____
5 He _____
6 He _____

3 Complete the information about the British Museum with *for* or *since*.

The British Museum has been open (0) ___*since*___ 1759, and has been a popular tourist attraction (1) _____ more than 200 years. Some of the objects in the museum have been there (2) _____ it first opened, and many others have been on show in the same rooms (3) _____ the nineteenth century. However, many of the objects in the museum were brought to Britain from other countries, and some countries such as Greece have tried (4) _____ many years to get back some of these important works of art.

THE BRITISH MUSEUM

Exam practice: Reading and Writing Part 3 (b)

4 Complete the conversation between Beth and the assistant in a tourist information office in London. What does Beth say to the assistant? For questions 1-5, mark the correct letter A-H.

ASSISTANT: Hello, can I help you?
BETH: (0) _D_
ASSISTANT: Of course. What would you like to know?
BETH: (1) _____
ASSISTANT: Yes, you can take the number 24 or go on the underground.
BETH: (2) _____
ASSISTANT: Every day from 10 a.m. till 5.30 p.m. And it's free.
BETH: (3) _____
ASSISTANT: There's a restaurant and a snack bar as well.
BETH: (4) _____
ASSISTANT: I'm sorry, we don't sell them here, but they have them at the museum.
BETH: (5) _____
ASSISTANT: Enjoy your visit!

A We can have lunch there.
B Fine. When is the museum open?
C How far is it?
D Yes, please. I'd like some information about the British Museum.
E That's really good. Is there anywhere to eat inside?
F And have you got a guide book to the museum?
G Can I get there by bus?
H OK. I'll buy one there then.

11.2 Turn left at the traffic lights

Language practice

1 Circle the word that doesn't belong in each group. How is this word different?

0 walk   cycle   (sail)   drive
  You sail on water, not on a road

1 roundabout   crossroad   traffic lights   fire station
  _____

2 garage   bus station   platform   petrol station
  _____

3 stadium   skatepark   library   swimming pool
  _____

4 motorway   street   river   bridge
  _____

5 café   hotel   burger bar   coffee shop
  _____

2 Put the letters in the right order to complete the directions

0 Turn left at the ___roundabout___ .   NOBURAODUT
1 Go past the _____.   SUMEMU
2 Go over the _____.   IRREV
3 Turn right by the _____.   TRELPO TOINSAT
4 Go past the _____.   IRYBARL
5 And then you'll be at the _____! KASERTAKP

3 Choose the correct words to complete the directions. Where do they lead to?

0 Go straight (on) / past until you get to the bank.
1 *Turn* / *Take* the next right.
2 Go *over* / *on* the bridge.
3 *Take* / *Turn* left at the traffic lights.
4 It's *at* / *on* your right.
5 It's *opposite* / *between* the supermarket.

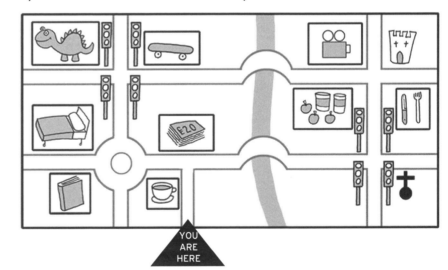

Exam practice: Reading and Writing Part 9

4 Read the email from your friend John.

To: _____
Subject: re: Next week

Hi there,
I'm staying in your town for a few days next week, and I'd really like to see you. When can we meet?
What shall we do together? Can you give me directions to your apartment?
John

5 Write an email to John. Answer the questions. Write 25-35 words

_____
_____
_____
_____
_____
_____
_____

12.1 I think technology is great

Language practice

1 Complete the crossword and find the hidden word.

1   This is the part of a TV you look at.

2   You use this to type.

3   You use this to send photos and messages to your friends.

4   You carry this in your pocket and use it to talk to people.

5   You do this when you look at lots of different websites.

6   The Simpsons is an example of this kind of programme.

7   You can play these on a console or on a computer.

8   A website where you can type messages to your friends.

2 Match the sentence halves.

0   I really like chatting
1   I often email
2   My brother spends a lot of time playing
3   You can find lots of interesting things by surfing
4   I often listen to
5   You shouldn't watch
6   I forgot to check

A   computer games.
B   music while I'm doing my homework.
C   photos to my grandma and granddad.
D   so many cartoons on TV!
E   my emails yesterday.
F   the internet.
G   to my friends online.

3 Look at the pictures. Write the correct sentence next to each picture.

She's looking at   She can see   She's watching   She's going to watch

0 *She can see* a boat

1 _____ TV.

2 _____ a coin.

3 _____ a film.

Exam practice: Reading and Writing Part 7

4 Complete this profile from a social networking website. Write ONE word for each space.

FACESPACE

Hello! My name's Sofia and I'm 14 **(0)** ____*years*____ old. I live at home

(1) _____ my parents and my brother Joey, who's a DJ. Joey and I like

(2) _____ of different kinds of music, including indie, pop **(3)** _____ hip-

hop. I write **(4)** _____ own songs too and I hope to study music at university

(5) _____ the future. I don't do much sport, but I'd like to try rock climbing

(6) _____ day. My favourite TV programmes **(7)** _____ Prison Break and

American Idol. I'm happiest when I'm having **(8)** _____ good time chatting to

my friends or listening **(9)** _____ music. I'm afraid **(10)** _____ insects

but I love animals – especially my cat, Shandy.

12.2 An amazing story

Language practice

1 Match the words with the descriptions.

0 You can find information about lots of different subjects.   A a textbook
1 You can find the meanings of words in this.   B a newspaper
2 You can read cartoons in this.   C a dictionary
3 This book tells a long story.   D a magazine
4 This tells you what is happening in the world every day.   E a comic
5 You can often read about famous people in this.   F a novel
6 You use this to learn from at school.   G an encyclopaedia

2 Complete the email with the correct form of the verbs. Use the past simple or the past continuous.

> **To:** Tom
>
> **Subject:** re: Grass?
>
> Hi Tom,
> I **(0)** _was walking_ (walk) home last night when I
> **(1)** _____ (see) something strange.
> Two men **(2)** _____ (wait) outside the bank.
> They **(3)** _____ (wear) dark clothes and when they
> **4)** _____ (see) me they **(5)** _____ (run)
> away. Do you think I should tell the police?
>
> John

Exam practice: Reading and Writing Part 5

3 Read the article about Moko the dolphin. Choose the best word
(A, B or C) for each space.

A Dolphin Hero

Early one morning **(0)** _____ March 2008, a mother and baby whale got into trouble at Mahia beach in New Zealand. Malcolm Smith and a team **(1)** _____ animal workers tried to push the whales back out to sea, **(2)** _____ they kept coming back onto **(3)** _____ beach. 'They were getting tired and I was afraid they were going to die,' said Malcolm. But then Moko the dolphin **(4)** _____.

Moko is well known at Mahia beach, **(5)** _____ she plays with swimmers and pushes boats along with **(6)** _____ nose. 'She came straight to us and then showed the two whales how to get away from the beach and out to open sea,' said Malcolm. 'It was a wonderful thing to watch.' No one has **(7)** _____ heard of a dolphin helping whales like this before, and **(8)** _____ agrees that Moko is a very special animal.

0 (A) in	B on	C at	5 A where	B who	C what
1 A by	B to	C of	6 A her	B their	C your
2 A or	B so	C but	7 A yet	B ever	C since
3 A the	B a	C one	8 A someone	B everyone	C anyone
4 A arrive	B arriving	C arrived			

Reading and Writing Paper

Part 1

Questions 1–5

Which notice **(A–H)** says this **(1–5)**?
For questions **1–5**, mark the correct letter **A–H** on your answer sheet.

Example:

0	All the students in the school can watch this.	*Answer:*	**0**	A B C D E F G H

---

1 You cannot wear shoes here.

A
> **Book sale**
> Tuesday after school in the school hall

2 You cannot take these into the classroom with you.

B
> *No Art classes today*
> *Mrs Smith is ill*

C
> Please clean your shoes before
> you come into the classroom

3 This person will not be at school today.

D
> *School play by 3S*
> *10.00am Friday*
> *Everyone welcome!*

4 You should read these here.

E
> School Trip
> Pay Mr Hart by Friday at the latest

5 You will be able to buy something here.

F
> Leave mobile phones with the
> school secretary during the day.

G
> Trainers or socks only in
> the sports hall please

H
> Books on this shelf must not
> be taken from the library

Part 2

Questions 6–10

Read the sentences about a shopping trip.
Choose the best word (**A**, **B** or **C**) for each space.
For questions **6–10**, mark **A**, **B** or **C** on your answer sheet.

Example:

0   On Saturday afternoons, Mariella usually .... shopping with her friend Jessica.

    A   goes   **B**   makes   **C**   takes   *Answer:*

0	A B C
	■ ☐ ☐

---

6   They don't spend much money but they love .... on clothes and shoes.

    A   getting   **B**   turning   **C**   trying

7   Last week Jessica bought a .... of sunglasses with her pocket money.

    A   bit   **B**   pair   **C**   piece

8   Sometimes they go to a music store and listen to the most .... CDs.

    A   nice   **B**   favourite   **C**   popular

9   The shop assistants don't .... if Jessica and Mariella don't buy anything.

    A   mind   **B**   like   **C**   want

10   Afterwards they go to a coffee shop and chat for a .... time.

    A   big   **B**   busy   **C**   long

Part 3

Questions 11–15

Complete the five conversations.
For questions **11–15**, mark **A**, **B** or **C** on your answer sheet.

Example:

0

How are you?

A	I'm Veronika.
B	I'm fine.
C	I'm ready.

Answer:

0	A B C
	☐ ■ ☐

---

11 What are you doing at the weekend?

    A I don't know yet.
    B I didn't on Sunday.
    C I'll finish it later.

12 It's a beautiful day.

    A I hope so.
    B Let's go swimming.
    C Do you know?

13 How long is the film?

    A Half past nine.
    B In twenty minutes.
    C Over two hours.

14 Do you have to wear a school uniform?

    A I never liked it
    B I don't, do you?
    C I don't want to.

15 Sorry I forgot your birthday.

    A Don't worry about it.
    B I can't remember.
    C I never know.

Questions 16–20

Complete the conversation between two friends.
What does Gina say to Philip?
For questions **16–20**, mark the correct letter **A–H** on your answer sheet.

Example:

Philip: I enjoyed the film, did you?

Gina: **0**   ...G....

Answer: | **0** | A B C D E F G H |

Philip: I'm hungry. How about going in this pizza restaurant?

Gina: **16** ....

Philip: OK. These pizzas look really good.

Gina: **17** ....

Philip: You can ask the cook not to put any on your pizza.

Gina: **18** ....

Philip: Well, how about just having an ice cream?

Gina: **19** ....

Philip: Are you sure that's OK?

Gina: **20** ....

Philip: Well, thanks a lot.

A   But they've all got onions on and I don't like onions.

B   I'd like one with tomato and cheese.

C   No, I don't like it.

D   Of course. I'll call her now and tell her we're coming.

E   Too cold. Let's just go back to my house. I'll ask Mum to make us some sandwiches.

F   Wait a minute. Let's look at the menu outside first.

G   It was great. What shall we do now?

H   I know, but I think it's going to be too expensive.

Part 4

Questions 21–27

Read the article about a sportsman.
Are sentences **21–27** 'Right' **(A)** or 'Wrong' **(B)**? If there is not enough information to answer 'Right' **(A)** or 'Wrong' **(B)**, choose 'Doesn't say' **(C)**.
For questions **21–27**, mark **A** , **B** or **C** on your answer sheet.

Jon Willis

Jon Willis is Britain's number 1 fencer. Our journalist Sarah Shephard met him and asked him a few questions.

Jon, when did you first start fencing?

I first tried the sport at an after-school club when I was 12. I didn't know anything about it, but it only cost £1.00 to have a lesson so I decided to try it.

Is it as dangerous as it looks?

There are actually very few fencing accidents. The most important thing is to wear the right clothes and to look after them well.

What makes you so good at your sport?

My fencing style is a bit different from other fencers and some people are surprised by this. Also, I work hard to be the best. A lot of other fencers are much less fit than I am.

What do you think you will do in the future?

I'm not sure. I've never had a job in my life! But I went to university before I became a fencer, so I suppose I might work for a big company one day. But at the moment I prefer the idea of being a teacher or a fire fighter.

Example:

0   Jon Willis is the best fencer in Britain.

    A   Right   **B**   Wrong   **C**   Doesn't say   *Answer:* **0** A B C

---

21   Jon joined the after-school club because he was very interested in fencing.

    A   Right   **B**   Wrong   **C**   Doesn't say

22   Jon says that people often get hurt when they are fencing.

    A   Right   **B**   Wrong   **C**   Doesn't say

23   Jon spends a lot of money buying the right fencing clothes.

    A   Right   **B**   Wrong   **C**   Doesn't say

24   Jon says he fences in an unusual way.

    A   Right   **B**   Wrong   **C**   Doesn't say

25   Jon thinks that he is fitter than most other fencers.

    A   Right   **B**   Wrong   **C**   Doesn't say

26   Jon worked for a big company after he left university.

    A   Right   **B**   Wrong   **C**   Doesn't say

27   Jon studied sports science at university.

    A   Right   **B**   Wrong   **C**   Doesn't say

Part 5

Questions 28–35

Read this text about the first films.
Choose the best word (**A**, **B** or **C**) for each space.
For questions **28–35**, mark **A**, **B** or **C** on your answer sheet.

The First Films

The brothers Louis and Auguste Lumiere were the first people in **(0)** .... world to make moving pictures. On December 28th 1895, in Paris, **(28)** .... showed a 'movie' in a cinema for the first time using a machine **(29)** .... the Cinematographe.

The film was a comedy about a gardener **(30)** .... had an accident with some water and got very wet. **(31)** .... thought it was very funny.

In 1907, the first film studios were built in a part **(32)** .... Los Angeles known as Hollywood. During the 1920s, Hollywood **(33)** .... the centre of the world film industry. In the beginning, the films had no sound. Instead, **(34)** .... were words on the screen **(35)** .... time to time, telling people the story.

Example:

0	**A**	a	**B**	one	**C**	the	*Answer:*	0	A B C □ □ ■

28	**A**	they	**B**	it	**C**	he
29	**A**	called	**B**	calling	**C**	calls
30	**A**	what	**B**	where	**C**	who
31	**A**	Someone	**B**	Anyone	**C**	Everyone
32	**A**	of	**B**	by	**C**	from
33	**A**	is	**B**	was	**C**	be
34	**A**	here	**B**	these	**C**	there
35	**A**	by	**B**	from	**C**	after

Part 6

Questions 36–40

Read the descriptions of some words about going to the beach.
What is the word for each one?
The first letter is already there. There is one space for each other letter in the word.
For questions **36–40**, write the words on your answer sheet.

Example:

0   You may take this to read on the beach.   b _ _ _

0	book

---

36   If you go swimming, you will need this to get dry afterwards.   t _ _ _ _

37   This is useful to lie under if the sun is too hot.   u _ _ _ _ _ _ _

38   This is a good game to play on the beach with a group of friends.   v _ _ _ _ _ _ _ _

39   You can go to this place if you are hungry or thirsty.   c _ _ _

40   You can sometimes rent this and go on the water in it.   b _ _ _

Part 7

Questions 41–50

Complete this email.
Write ONE word for each space.
For questions **41–50**, write the words on your answer sheet.

Example: | **0** | had |

| **From:** | Jim |
| **To:** | Tony |

Jim,

I hope you **(0)** .... a good time at my party last night. I really enjoyed it!
Thanks very much **(41)** .... the computer game you bought me. I play with it
(42) .... the time.

I got some good presents **(43)** .... my parents too. My Dad gave me a
skateboard. It's bigger **(44)** .... my old one and it's **(45)** .... a really cool
picture on the bottom.

Would you **(46)** .... to come and try it? I'm free **(47)** .... Thursday after
school. My Mum says we **(48)** .... to do our homework first, but **(49)** ....
will be time to go to the park afterwards. Call me and let me know **(50)** ....
you can come.

Tony

Part 8

Questions 51–55

Read the advertisement and the email.
Fill in the information in Helena's notes.
For questions **51–55**, write the information on your answer sheet.

ADVENTURE WORLD

Open from March 14th
to October 31st

Free shows – 2pm and 4pm daily

Prices

Over 12 – £24.00
Under 12 – £16.00

From:	Gabi
To:	Helena

Good news! Dad says he'll take us to Adventure World on May 21st! Mum needs the car that day, so we'll take the train. It will be more expensive this year because we are 13, but never mind! Bring your camera but don't worry about sandwiches – we'll buy food there.
See you at school tomorrow.

Helena's Notes

Trip to: Adventure World

Date: **51** _____

Price per person: **52** _____

First show starts at: **53** _____

Travel there by: **54** _____

What to take: **54** _____

Part 9

Question 56

Read this email from your friend Billy.

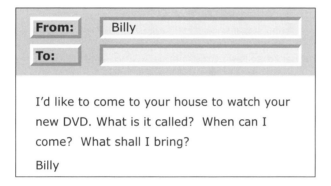

From: Billy

To:

I'd like to come to your house to watch your new DVD. What is it called? When can I come? What shall I bring?

Billy

Write Billy an email and answer the questions.
Write **25–35** words.
Write the email on your answer sheet.

Listening Paper

 01 [CD-ROM]

Part 1

Questions 1–5

You will hear five short conversations.
You will hear each conversation twice.
There is one question for each conversation.
For each question, choose the right answer (**A**, **B** or **C**).

Example: How many people were at the party?

3	**13**	**30**
A	B	Ⓒ

---

1 What sport does Joseph do?

A	B	C

---

2 What time will the girls meet?

A	B	C

3 How will Mary get to school today?

 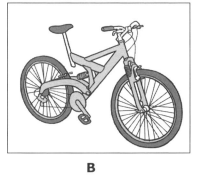 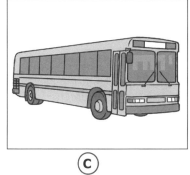

A B C

4 What did the boy buy?

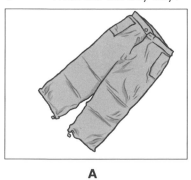 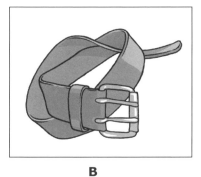 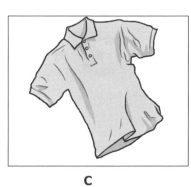

A B C

5 What will Lily have for lunch?

A B C

02 [CD-ROM]

Part 2

Questions 6–10

Listen to Robert talking to Katy about her room.
Where do they decide to put Katy's things?
For questions **6–10**, write a letter **(A–H)** next to each thing.
You will hear the conversation twice.

Example:

0   computer | C |

THINGS		PLACES	
6 dictionaries	☐	**A**	bed
		B	big cupboard
7 pillow	☐	**C**	desk
		D	floor
8 plant	☐	**E**	shelf
9 photograph	☐	**F**	small cupboard
		G	sofa
10 toy bear	☐	**H**	table

Part 3

Questions 11–15

Listen to Fiona talking to Mark about her new bike.
For each question, choose the right answer (**A**, **B** or **C**).
You will hear the conversation twice.

Example:

0   Fiona is getting her new bike

    A   this morning.

    B   tomorrow morning.

    (C)   tomorrow afternoon.

---

11   What kind of bike is Fiona getting?

    A   a racing bike

    B   a mountain bike

    C   a shopping bike

12   Fiona has bought her bike from

    A   a website.

    B   an advertisement in a newspaper.

    C   a shop selling bicycles.

13   Who is going to put Fiona's bike together?

    A   Fiona

    B   Mark

    C   Fiona's dad

14   Fiona and Mark will go for a bike ride to

    A   the beach.

    B   a wood.

    C   a field.

15   Mark will come for Fiona at

    A   9 a.m.

    B   9.30 a.m.

    C   10.30 a.m.

04 [CD-ROM]

Part 4

Questions 16–20

You will hear a girl asking for information about a summer camp.
Listen and complete each question.
You will hear the conversation twice.

Summer Camp

Name of camp:	Island Adventure
Nearest town:	**(16)** ....
Phone number:	**(17)** .... (for more information)
Cost for a week in July:	**(18)** £ ....
Sports:	**(19)** .... and water sports
Event on the last night:	**(20)** ....

---

05 [CD-ROM]

Part 5

Questions 21–25

You will hear a woman on the radio talking about a competition.
Listen and complete each question.
You will hear the information twice.

Art Competition

Name of programme:	The Picture Show
Artists must not be more than:	**(21)** ....
This year's subject:	**(22)** ....
First prize:	**(23)** ....
Competition address:	**(24)** 95 High Street, ...
Closing date for competition:	**(25)** ....

Speaking Paper

Part 1

The examiner will ask you some questions about you, your family and your life.

For example:

1   What's your name?
2   Where are you from?
3   What is your favourite subject at school?
4   What do you usually do at the weekend?
5   Tell me about your family. Do you have any brothers or sisters?

Part 2

The examiner will give you some cards. You need to ask and answer questions with your partner.

Student A

1   Here is some information about a zoo. Student B doesn't know anything about the zoo. Listen to Student B's questions and answer them.

SHELTON ZOO

HADSTOCK ROAD, SHELTON

OPEN DAILY

SUMMER 10 AM – 6PM

WINTER 10 AM – 4PM

COME AND SEE THE NEW BABY ELEPHANT!

ADVENTURE PLAYGROUND FOR CHILDREN

FAMILY TICKET: £20

2   Student B has some Information about a book. You don't know anything about the book, so ask Student B about it. Use these words to make your questions.

> **Book**
>
> - name ?
> - writer?
> - what / about ?
> - price?
> - where / buy?

Student B

1   Student A has some information about a zoo. You don't know anything about the zoo, so ask Student A about it. Use these words to make your questions.

Zoo

- where?
- what / see?
- when / open / summer ?
- tickets / expensive?
- children / play?

2   Here is some information about a book. Student A doesn't know anything about the book. Listen to Student A's questions and answer them.

Charles Weston

Living with Lions
Life in an African animal park

Comes out next month
£16.50 from all good bookshops next month
or online: www.lionsafari.com

Exam answer sheets

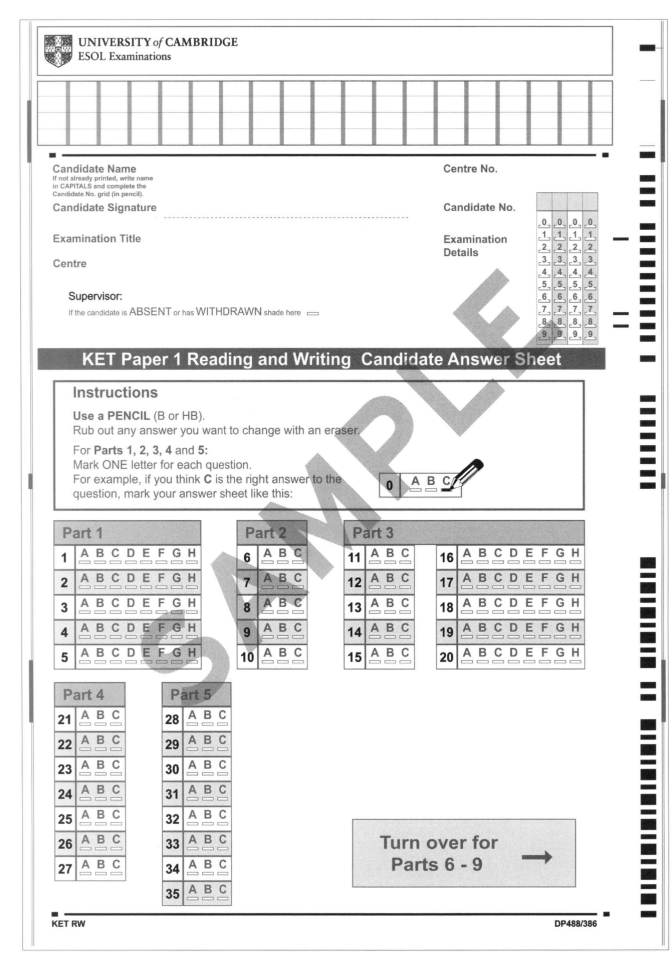

UNIVERSITY *of* CAMBRIDGE
ESOL Examinations

Candidate Name
If not already printed, write name in CAPITALS and complete the Candidate No. grid (in pencil).

Candidate Signature

Examination Title

Centre

Supervisor:
If the candidate is ABSENT or has WITHDRAWN shade here

Centre No.

Candidate No.

Examination Details

KET Paper 1 Reading and Writing Candidate Answer Sheet

Instructions

Use a PENCIL (B or HB).
Rub out any answer you want to change with an eraser.

For **Parts 1, 2, 3, 4** and **5:**
Mark ONE letter for each question.
For example, if you think **C** is the right answer to the question, mark your answer sheet like this:

0   A B C

Part 1

1	A B C D E F G H
2	A B C D E F G H
3	A B C D E F G H
4	A B C D E F G H
5	A B C D E F G H

Part 2

6	A B C
7	A B C
8	A B C
9	A B C
10	A B C

Part 3

11	A B C	16	A B C D E F G H
12	A B C	17	A B C D E F G H
13	A B C	18	A B C D E F G H
14	A B C	19	A B C D E F G H
15	A B C	20	A B C D E F G H

Part 4

21	A B C
22	A B C
23	A B C
24	A B C
25	A B C
26	A B C
27	A B C

Part 5

28	A B C
29	A B C
30	A B C
31	A B C
32	A B C
33	A B C
34	A B C
35	A B C

**Turn over for
Parts 6 - 9** →

KET RW   DP488/386

For **Parts 6, 7 and 8:**

Write your answers in the spaces next to the numbers (36 to 55) like this:

0	example

Part 6		Do not write here
36		1 36 0
37		1 37 0
38		1 38 0
39		1 39 0
40		1 40 0

Part 7		Do not write here
41		1 41 0
42		1 42 0
43		1 43 0
44		1 44 0
45		1 45 0
46		1 46 0
47		1 47 0
48		1 48 0
49		1 49 0
50		1 50 0

Part 8		Do not write here
51		1 51 0
52		1 52 0
53		1 53 0
54		1 54 0
55		1 55 0

Part 9 (Question 56): Write your answer below.

Do not write below (Examiner use only)					
0	1	2	3	4	5

SAMPLE

Reproduced with the permission of Cambridge ESOL.

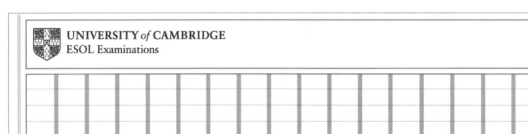

UNIVERSITY *of* CAMBRIDGE
ESOL Examinations

Candidate Name
If not already printed, write name
in CAPITALS and complete the
Candidate No. grid (in pencil).

Candidate Signature

Examination Title

Centre

Supervisor:
If the candidate is ABSENT or has WITHDRAWN shade here ⬜

Centre No.

Candidate No.

Examination Details

0	0	0	0
1	1	1	1
2	2	2	2
3	3	3	3
4	4	4	4
5	5	5	5
6	6	6	6
7	7	7	7
8	8	8	8
9	9	9	9

KET Paper 2 Listening Candidate Answer Sheet

Instructions

Use a PENCIL (B or HB).

Rub out any answer you want to change with an eraser.

For **Parts 1, 2** and **3**:
Mark ONE letter for each question.
For example, if you think **C** is the right answer to the
question, mark your answer sheet like this:

0	A B C

Part 1

1	A B C
2	A B C
3	A B C
4	A B C
5	A B C

Part 2

6	A B C D E F G H
7	A B C D E F G H
8	A B C D E F G H
9	A B C D E F G H
10	A B C D E F G H

Part 3

11	A B C
12	A B C
13	A B C
14	A B C
15	A B C

For **Parts 4** and **5**:
Write your answers in the spaces next to the
numbers (16 to 25) like this:

0	example

Part 4		Do not write here
16		1 16 0
17		1 17 0
18		1 18 0
19		1 19 0
20		1 20 0

Part 5		Do not write here
21		1 21 0
22		1 22 0
23		1 23 0
24		1 24 0
25		1 25 0

KET L

DP314/088

Reproduced with the permission of Cambridge ESOL.